The Desborough Cook Book

Compiled and edited by Fiona Barber
Illustrated by John Blackwell

Published by the Desborough Civic Society, Northamptonshire
Charity Register Number 1086882 (2009)

ISBN: 978-0-9563207-0-4

Printed by Phoenix Printing Company, Desborough.

Acknowledgments

The Desborough Civic Society of Northamptonshire would like to thank those people who have, directly or indirectly, kindly donated recipes in order to raise funds for the Desborough Heritage Centre.

Natalie Alderson-Smith
Phyllis Allen
Fiona Barber
Vivienne Barton
John Blackwell
Jennifer Blackwell
Sylvia Cank, for her recipes from when she was a chef at Cheaney's
Jenny Carr
Jill Freeman
Mrs Freer
Louise Gutteridge
Liz Harris
Jan Hollinshead
Bob Martin
Diana Smith
Sue Starmer
Mrs Turner

Thanks are also given to:

Fiona Barber for compiling the book
John Blackwell for illustrating the book
Belinda Humfrey for proof-reading the book

CONTENTS

Sections

Recipes

Cooking temperatures

Degrees Fahrenheit	Degrees Celsius	Gas Mark	Description
225	110	¼	Very Slow
250	120/130	½	Very Slow
275	140	1	Slow
300	150	2	Slow
325	160/170	3	Moderate
350	180	4	Moderate
375	190	5	Moderately Hot
400	200	6	Moderately Hot
425	220	7	Hot
450	230	8	Hot
475	240	9	Hot

Weights and measures

Imperial	Metric
½ oz	15g
1 oz	30g
4 oz	125g
8 oz	250g
12 oz	375g
1lb	500g

Cup and spoon sizes

Imperial measure	Metric measure
¼ teaspoon	1.25 ml
½ teaspoon	2.5 ml
1 teaspoon	5 ml
1 tablespoon	20 ml
¼ cup	60 ml
½ cup	125 ml
1 cup	250 ml

Liquids

Imperial	Cup	Metric
1 fl oz		30 ml
2 fl oz	¼ cup	60 ml
3 fl oz		100 ml
4 fl oz	½ cup	125 ml
6 fl oz	¾ cup	200 ml
8 fl oz	1 cup	250 ml

Please note: all oven temperatures given are approximate and may need to be adjusted to suit the oven being used

General Maxims for Health

Rise early. Eat simple food. Take plenty of exercise. Never fear a little fatigue. Let not children be dressed in tight clothes; it is necessary their limbs and muscles should have full play, if you wish for either health or beauty.

Avoid the necessity of a physician, if you can, by careful attention to your diet. Eat what best agrees with your system, and resolutely abstain from what hurts you, however well you may like it. A few days' abstinence, and cold water for a beverage, has driven off many an approaching disease.

If you find yourself really ill, send for a good physician. Have nothing to do with quacks; and do not tamper with quack medicine.

Mrs Childs, The Frugal Housewife, c.1925

Egg dishes

Alpine Eggs (serves three people)

6 large eggs
12oz (350g) cheddar cheese grated
1oz (25g) butter
salt and freshly milled black pepper

Garnish: 1 dessert spoon snipped fresh chives

Preheat oven to Gas mark 4/350F/180C

1. Generously butter a shallow oval baking dish, and then cover with half of the grated cheese.
2. Carefully break the eggs onto the cheese (make a slight indentation), season well, and then sprinkle the rest of the cheese over the eggs, covering them completely.
3. Dot with a few flecks of butter and bake in the centre of the oven for 15 minutes, by which time the eggs will have set and the cheese be bubbling and melted.
4. To serve, sprinkle with chives, serve with crusty bread and side salad.

For special occasions serve Alpine Eggs as a first course.
Use individual ramekin dishes, buttered with one egg per person and 2oz of gruyere cheese. Cook as above.

Asparagus Soufflé (serves 4)

2oz butter
2oz plain flour
½ pint milk
10oz can green asparagus tips
3 eggs
½ teaspoon made English mustard
1oz grated cheddar cheese
grated rind of ½ a lemon
salt and black pepper

Preheat oven to Gas mark 5/375F/190C

1. Melt butter in a saucepan, stir in flour and cook gently for one minute to form a smooth paste.
2. Add milk slowly, beating to keep mixture smooth.
3. Bring to the boil and cook for three minutes, stirring continuously.
4. Drain asparagus tips, chop and add to the white sauce with the mustard and grated cheese.
5. Separate eggs and beat yolks into the mixture. Add seasoning and lemon rind.
6. Beat the egg whites stiffly and fold into the mixture.
7. Pour into buttered 2 pint soufflé dish.
8. Stand soufflé dish in a pan of hot water whilst baking for 45 minutes.
9. Serve immediately.

Cream Eggs (serves four)

3 hard boiled eggs
3 oz cooked ham, finely diced
1 small green pepper, de-seeded and diced
¼ pint double cream
3 tablespoons mayonnaise
pinch of curry powder
salt and pepper
crispy lettuce hearts

Garnish: paprika pepper and chopped parsley

1. Hard boil the eggs for ten minutes and put in cold water to cool, remove shells and chop the whole eggs.
2. Whisk cream in a bowl until it holds its shape; add the mayonnaise and curry powder and seasoning. Fold in the eggs, chopped ham and peppers.
3. Shred the lettuce hearts finely, arrange in four individual bowls, pile on the egg mixture and sprinkle with paprika and chopped parsley.

Eggy Bread (serves four)

3 eggs
2 tablespoons of milk (optional)
salt and pepper
4 thick slices of white bread
butter for frying
tomato or brown sauce according to taste

1. Beat together the eggs, milk, preferred sauce, salt and pepper.
2. Cut the bread into quarters, soak each piece of bread in the mixture and coat well.
3. Heat the butter in a large frying pan and fry soaked bread squares until golden brown, turning once. Any spare egg mixture should be poured over the bread as it is fried.
4. Serve with crispy bacon.

Hot Cheese Stuffed Eggs (serves 4)

4 hard boiled eggs (shelled)
2 oz softened butter
2 oz grated cheese
one clove garlic crushed with a little salt (optional)
pinch of salt and cayenne pepper to taste
tablespoon of cream

Cheese sauce
1oz butter
1oz flour
½ pint milk
2oz grated cheese

Garnish: 8 cooked mushroom caps

1. Cut the eggs length wise, remove yolks and mash with a fork; add softened butter, grated cheese, garlic, seasoning and cream; mix well.
2. Divide the mixture equally between the halved eggs piling smoothly, and place into a small oven-proof dish or individual ramekin dishes.
3. Make the cheese sauce and coat the eggs.
4. Sprinkle with extra grated cheese and brown under a hot grill.
5. Garnish with cooked mushrooms and serve hot.

Mariner's Omelette (serves 2 – 3 people)

4 eggs beaten
1 fillet smoked haddock
3oz cheddar cheese
black pepper

Preheat oven to Gas mark 4/350F/180C

1. Beat the eggs together in a bowl.
2. Remove the haddock skin and discard; cut the flesh into small pieces.
3. Dice the cheese similarly.
4. Put the fish and cheese into the beaten egg, season with pepper and mix well.
5. Grease a shallow oven proof dish, pour in the egg mixture and bake for 5 - 10 minutes until bubbling hot and the cheese is melted.
6. Serve on its own as a supper dish or with mashed potatoes and salad for a more substantial lunch.

Cakes

Apple Scones (makes about 30)

The secret to making a good scone is to use butter, never margarine and not making them too big. Sylvia Cank.

900g SR flour
225g butter, cubed
225g caster sugar
2 bramley apples grated (you can leave the peel on)
300ml milk
5 tablespoons demerara sugar

Preheat oven to Gas mark 7/425F/220C

1. Put flour into a large bowl, add butter and rub lightly until the mixture resembles coarse crumbs; stir in the sugar and the apples.
2. Add 250ml of milk and mix to form a soft dough.
3. Turn out onto a floured board and gently shape into a flat disc, 2.5cm thick.
4. Cut scones with 5cm cutter.
5. Transfer to a non-stick baking sheet.
6. Brush the tops with remaining milk and sprinkle each scone with Demerara sugar.
7. Bake in the centre of the oven for 12–15 minutes until well risen and golden brown.
8. Leave to cool slightly; serve warm with butter, jam or cream.
9. Eat within 24 hours.

Barm Brack

This recipe was a favourite of Mrs Phyllis Allen (née Gooch) of Pioneer Avenue, Desborough. She passed the recipe on to her friends, in the 1970s. Liz Harris.

8 oz mixed fruit
4 oz margarine
3 oz sugar
6 oz SR flour
1 egg
1 teaspoon bicarbonate of soda
1 cup boiling water

Preheat the oven Gas 6/400F/200C

1. Rub fat into sugar and flour.
2. Add egg, fruit and bicarbonate of soda to boiling water; stir. (It looks like a mess for a mad dog but tastes good.)
3. Bake for 45 mins to one hour.

Boiled Cider and Fruit Cake

This cake was used as a celebration cake after WW 2 (late 40s and early 50s) when rationing became easier. Sylvia Cank.

4oz margarine
6oz brown sugar
10oz mixed dried fruit
8 fl. oz cider
1 heaped teaspoon mixed spice
2 eggs
8oz SR flour

Preheat oven to Gas mark 4/350F/180C

1. Put margarine, sugar, fruit, cider and mixed spice into a pan, bring to the boil, then allow to cool.
2. When cool, add beaten eggs and flour.
3. Mix well and pour into a lined 8" round cake tin.
4. Bake in the centre of the oven for approximately 1¼ hours. Leave in the tin to cool.
5. It will keep up to four weeks in an airtight container.

Custard Creams

2oz margarine
3 tablespoons custard powder
3 tablespoons sugar
3 tablespoons SR flour
1 egg beaten

Preheat oven to Gas mark 5/375F/190C

Lightly grease and flour a flat baking sheet.

1. Mix all dry ingredients together.
2. Rub in margarine.
3. Mix to a stiff paste using as much of the egg as is needed.
4. Rest mixture in the fridge for ½ hour.
5. Roll out to ¼ inch thick; cut with small round cutter.
6. Bake in a moderate oven. Do not let them brown.
7. When cool, sandwich together with butter-cream icing.

Date and Fruit Cake (suitable for diabetics)

2oz sultanas
2oz currants
2oz stoned dates
2oz margarine
¼ pint semi-skimmed milk

Preheat oven to Gas mark 4/350F/180C

1. Put all ingredients into a saucepan and bring to the boil. Simmer for 10 minutes and leave to cool.
2. Line a 7" deep cake tin.

Then add

5oz SR flour
2 teaspoons nutmeg
2 teaspoons cinnamon
1 teaspoon baking powder

3. Add gradually to the cooled mixture and stir thoroughly. If required add a little more milk, until mixture is 'soft dropping' in consistency.
4. Bake for 45 minutes to 1 hour, or until a skewer inserted comes out clean.
5. Leave in the tin to cool.

Ginger Cookies (makes 30)

1 cup sugar
1 cup porridge oats
1 cup SR flour
4oz margarine
1 tablespoon syrup
½ level teaspoon bicarbonate of soda
½ level teaspoon ground ginger

Preheat oven to Gas mark 4/350F/180C

1. Put all dry ingredients into a bowl; mix well.
2. Melt margarine and syrup in a saucepan over a low heat.
3. Pour in the dry ingredients; mix well.
4. Using a teaspoon of mixture at a time, roll into balls and place well apart on a greased baking sheet.
5. Cook for 5 – 6 minutes until golden brown.
6. Leave to cool slightly before transferring to a cooling rack.

Ginger Layer Cake

This recipe was taken from the Stanion Cookery Book of the 1920s; the recipe was given by Mrs Freer formerly of Desborough.

½ breakfast cup of flour
¾ breakfast cup of caster sugar
whites of 6 eggs
8 drops vanilla essence
1 teaspoon cream of tartar

Preheat oven to Gas mark 3-4/325 - 350F/160-180C (moderate oven)

1. Beat the egg whites and sugar to a cream.
2. Add the flour and cream of tartar.
3. Bake for 20-30 minutes.

Filling
1 teaspoon cornflour
¾ teacup of sugar
beaten yolks of 3 eggs
1 teacup boiling milk

4. Stir over a fire until the mixture thickens; flavour with vanilla.
5. Split the cake into 3 layers and spread each layer with the filling, adding in layers of preserved ginger.
6. Top off with icing.

Great Granny's Plum Bread

2lb SR flour
½ oz yeast
1lb soft brown sugar
2lb mixed dried fruit
¼ lb glace cherries
¼ lb mixed peel
1 pint of milk
½ teaspoon salt
½ lb butter

Preheat oven to Gas mark 3/325F/160-170C

1. Rub butter into flour.
2. Add all dry ingredients and mix well.
3. Slightly warm the milk and mix half with the yeast and half with the beaten eggs.
4. Beat all ingredients together.
5. Bake in greased lined loaf tins (makes 1 large or 2 small loaves).
6. Bake large loaves for 2 hours, the small ones for 1½ hours.
7. It will keep in a tin for up to 3 months and is suitable for freezing.

Hazelnut Cheese Cake

This dish was given to me about 12 years ago; I have made it many times as it is so quick and easy and failsafe! Natalie Alderson-Smith (The Cabbage Patch fruit and veg shop)

Base
8 oz digestive biscuits crushed
4 oz melted butter

1. Mix melted margarine and crushed biscuits together.
2. Grease a flan dish; line with biscuit mix.
3. Place in the fridge.

Filling
10oz hazelnut yoghurt
6oz cream cheese e.g. Philadelphia
½ pint double cream
4 oz caster sugar

1. Mix together cream cheese and sugar; beat well.
2. Whip double cream until thick.
3. Add yoghurt to cream cheese; mix well.
4. Add in the whipped cream; mix well.
5. Spoon mixture into the lined flan dish; smooth the top.
6. Decorate with grated chocolate or hazelnuts.
7. Place in the fridge to set.

Hertfordshire Tea Loaf

1 lb mixed fruit
¼ lb glace cherries
½ lb brown sugar
1½ cups cold tea (14 fl oz)

} soak overnight

Then add
2 eggs
1 lb SR flour

Preheat oven to Gas mark 3/325F/160-170C

Line two 1 lb loaf tins (or one 2lb tin)

1. Mix thoroughly the mixture soaked overnight; then add the beaten eggs and fold in the flour.
2. Pour the mix into the loaf tin/s.
3. Cook slowly for approximately 1¼ hours, or until well risen and a skewer, when inserted into the centre, comes out clean.
4. Cook on a wire rack.
5. When cold, slice and spread with butter.
6. If wrapped in foil it will keep for 2 – 3 days, suitable for freezing.

Lemon Caraway Cake

Very good. Sylvia Cank.

8oz SR flour
6oz butter
4oz caster sugar
5 tablespoons lemon curd
pinch of salt
3 eggs
1 level teaspoon of caraway seeds

Preheat oven to Gas mark 3/325F/160-170C

1. Cream butter, sugar and lemon curd until light.
2. Beat in the salt and the eggs one at a time.
3. Add the flour and caraway seed.
4. Grease and flour a 7" tin and bake in the centre of the oven for one hour to one hour 10 minutes.

Light Fatless Sponge Cake

The weight of two large eggs in SR flour and sugar
1 large tablespoon of boiling water

Preheat oven to Gas mark 4/350F/180C

1. Grease a round sponge tin.
2. Whisk well the eggs and sugar.
3. Fold in the flour lightly.
4. Add one tablespoon of fast-boiling water.
5. Bake for half an hour.

Royal Raisin Squares

Pastry
6oz plain flour
pinch salt
1½ oz lard
1½ oz margarine
little water to bind dough

Filling
6oz seedless raisins
2oz cake crumbs (Madeira type)
1 egg yolk
grated rind of ½ lemon

Topping
8oz sifted icing sugar
1 egg white
squeeze lemon juice
redcurrant jelly (optional)

Preheat oven to Gas mark 5/375F/190C

1. Make pastry; rest it for 20 minutes, then roll it out and line a 7" square tin.
2. Put raisins, cake crumbs and lemon rind into a basin; bind them together with egg yolk.
3. Turn mix into the pastry case and level the surface.
4. Mix icing sugar, egg white and lemon juice; pour this over the filling.
5. Pipe lattice work of redcurrant jelly over the top (optional).
6. Bake for approximately ½ hour. Reduce the oven temperature to Gas 4 (350F/180C) for a further 10 minutes.
7. Leave to cool, then slice into squares.

Scottish Shortbread

These next two recipes were given to me whilst I was working in Scotland during 2008; they are quick, easy and delicious. Fiona Barber.

½ lb slightly salted butter
9oz plain flour
3oz corn flour
3oz castor sugar plus extra for dusting

Preheat oven to Gas mark 4/350F/180C

1. Sift dry ingredients together.
2. Melt butter in a pan over stove or in a bowl in the microwave.
3. Once melted, mix dry ingredients and stir well. The mixture should form a soft dough.
4. Tip into a Swiss roll tin and spread evenly; prick all over with a fork.
5. Bake 45 minutes to one hour until golden on the top.
6. Remove from oven and immediately cut into fingers with a sharp knife and dust with sugar.
7. Remove from tin when cool.

Scottish Tablet

You'll need a large bowl due to a very lively bubbling mixture….

1lb caster sugar
small tin Carnation milk (evaporated rather than condensed)
2oz butter

1. Mix all ingredients together in bowl and microwave for 4 minutes.
2. Stir.
3. Microwave for another 4 minutes.
4. Stir.
5. Microwave for another 4 minutes.
6. Stir until the candy sticks to the side of the bowl. (This happens pretty quickly.)
7. Pour into a small greased tin; leave to cool.

You need to act on points 6 and 7 very quickly, because of the fast setting. It helps if there are two of you, one to hold the bowl, one to scrape!

Desserts

Banoffee Trifle

This is a really quick, mostly store cupboard dessert, but a real favourite with the children. Fiona Barber.

1 banana instant whip
1 butterscotch instant whip
1 raspberry jam Swiss roll
2 bananas
1 jar of toffee sauce (the sort that is used for pouring over ice cream)
1 chocolate flake

1. Slice the Swiss roll and arrange in the bottom of the serving bowl.
2. Slice the bananas and arrange over the Swiss roll.
3. Pour over the jar of toffee sauce.
4. Whip one of the instant whips and pour over the fruit layer.
5. Whip the second instant whip and pour over the first one. Pour slowly to stop the two mixing together.
6. Break up the chocolate flake and sprinkle over the top of the trifle.
7. A layer of cream may be added before the flake, if required.
8. It is best eaten on the day it is made.

Boiled Batter Pudding

3 eggs
1 pint milk
½ teaspoon salt
1oz butter
3 tablespoons SR flour

1. Put the flour in a bowl; make a well in the centre, break in the eggs and salt and gradually mix, adding the milk until the batter is free of lumps and all the milk is used.
2. Place in a well-buttered pudding basin, leaving room to rise.
3. Cover and place in a saucepan of boiling water to come half way up the basin.
4. Boil for 1¼ hours.
5. Serve immediately, traditionally served with butter and sugar, or if preferred, stewed fruit, jam or sweet sauce.

Cream (excellent for large charity parties)

¼ level teaspoon gelatine
¼ lb unsalted butter
¼ pint milk
2 level teaspoons sugar

1. Place gelatine in a bowl with a teaspoon of water.
2. Cut up the butter and put in a small saucepan with milk; stir over the low heat until the butter has melted.
3. Pour on the gelatine mixture and stir briskly; pour into a liquidiser goblet.
4. Add sugar and run the machine on high for 30 seconds.
5. Pour in a bowl or plastic container; leave to cool.
6. Place in a refrigerator and leave for several hours or overnight.
7. This cream may be whisked until stiff or used for pouring.

Duke of Cambridge Tart

Flan
4oz SR flour
1oz margarine
1oz lard
pinch of salt
water to bind

Filling
2oz chopped cherries
2oz raisins
3oz butter
3oz caster sugar
2 egg yolks
1 tablespoon of sherry

Preheat oven to Gas mark 2/300F/150C

1. Make the pastry and prepare the flan case.
2. Melt the butter in saucepan; add sugar and stir until dissolved.
3. Add the slightly-beaten yolks and bring to the boil.
4. Remove from the heat and add the sherry and dried fruits.
5. Pour into the flan case and bake for 40 minutes.
6. Serve cold with cream.

Family Pudding

A very old and well tried recipe. Sylvia Cank.

5oz SR flour
3oz white bread crumbs
5oz sugar
¼ lb suet
½ lb sultanas
2oz candied peel
1 egg
a few drops of vanilla essence
milk, sufficient to mix

1. Mix all the dry ingredients together.
2. Add the beaten egg and sufficient milk to bind.
3. Put the mixture into a greased basin and boil for 1 – 1½ hours.

Friar's Omelette (serves 4)

The name of this dish is nothing to do with a churchman but is a corruption of 'fraise', the medieval version of an omelette. It is in fact, a very early version of apple charlotte. Sylvia Cank.

2 large beaten eggs
1lb cooking apples, peeled, cored and sliced
3oz butter
3oz soft brown sugar
rind of half a lemon with a teaspoon of lemon juice
or
½ teaspoon of nutmeg
4oz fresh white breadcrumbs

Preheat oven to Gas mark 5/375F/190C

1. Butter a 1½ to 2 pint pie dish.
2. Cook together the apples, butter, sugar, lemon rind and juice (or nutmeg) in a saucepan until soft, then beat to a thick purée.
3. Remove from the heat and stir in the beaten eggs.
4. Spread half the breadcrumbs on the base of the pie dish, spread over the apple mixture; then top with the remaining breadcrumbs. Dot with butter and sprinkle with a little extra sugar.
5. Bake for 30 - 40 minutes.
6. Serve hot with custard or whipped cream.

Farmhouse Tart

This is a very old recipe, but can be converted to use convenient items to make it as a 'quickie' all-in-one dessert. Sylvia Cank.

1 packet ready-to-roll shortcrust pastry
strawberry jam
1 lb bramley apples (or similar)
1 carton readymade custard

Preheat oven to Gas mark 4/350F/180C

1. Lightly roll out pastry and line an 8" tin approx 1½ "deep.
2. Blind bake for 15 minutes; remove beans and paper and return to the oven for approx 15 minutes, until the pastry is dry.
3. Peel, core and slice the apples; cook them in a small amount of water until tender, with sugar to taste. Leave to cool. Drain off any excess liquid.
4. Spread the base of the pastry case with strawberry jam, or a jam of your choice.
5. Layer with apples; finally pour over the ready-made custard.
6. Leave in the fridge to set.

Ginger Log

1 packet of ginger-nut biscuits
½ pint double cream
2 tablespoons sherry
small tin pineapple
glacé cherries

1. Whip cream and put aside.
2. Mix pineapple juice and sherry in a shallow dish and dip biscuits in one at a time; remove and sandwich together with the cream to form a log on a serving dish.
3. Cover the log with the remaining cream and decorate with the pineapple and cherries.

Hungarian Apple Pie

Pastry
6oz SR flour
1 egg yolk
4oz butter or margarine
2 tablespoons milk

Filling
4 tablespoons apricot jam
2oz ground hazelnuts
1 lb unsweetened stewed apple
2 tablespoons caster sugar
1 egg white

Preheat oven to Gas mark 6/400F/200C

1. Rub butter into flour; mix with egg yolk and milk. Roll out and use 2/3 of the pastry to line an 8" flan tin.
2. Spread the base with jam.
3. Sprinkle with half the nuts and sugar.
4. Beat the egg white until stiff, fold into the apple.
5. Spoon the apple mixture over the nuts and sugar; then sprinkle with the rest of the nuts and sugar.
6. Cover with the remaining pastry.
7. Bake for 25 minutes.

Lemon and Lime Cream Pie

200g / 7oz ginger nuts or digestives
75g / 3oz butter, melted
2 large limes
3 large lemons
1 x 405g tin condensed milk
1 x 284ml carton whipping cream

1. Mix biscuits and butter together and press into a 8" flan tin to line base and sides; chill.
   (For a firmer crust bake 375/190/Gas 5 for 10 minutes.)
2. Grate zest from one lime and one lemon. Squeeze the remaining lime and lemons to give 175ml/6 fl oz juice.
3. Place the zest, juice, condensed milk and cream in bowl. Whisk until lightly thickened.
4. Pour into the base and chill for at least two hours.
5. Decorate with lemon and lime slices.

Lemon Layer Pudding

2 large lemons
5oz caster sugar
½ pint milk
2 large eggs
1½ oz flour (either)
2oz butter

Preheat oven to Gas mark 4/350F/180C

1. Grate the rind of the lemons, avoiding all traces of the pith.
2. Beat the egg yolks, sugar, butter, flour, milk and five tablespoons of lemon juice, and the rind, until smooth.
3. In another bowl whisk the egg whites until stiff; fold other ingredients into the whites, a little at a time.
4. Turn the mixture into a buttered two-pint oven-proof dish.
5. Place in a roasting tin with water half-way up the sides for 45 minutes, until golden and lightly set. Serve hot.

N.B. when baked this pudding has a sponge-like top and a lemon curd texture below. No cream or custard is needed.

Northamptonshire Cheesecake
(sufficient to make 16 small cakes or a 9" cake)

8oz curd cheese or cottage cheese
2oz butter
2 eggs
3oz caster sugar
4oz dried mixed fruit
2 lemons (grated rind)
pinch of nutmeg
a few drops of almond essence
8oz shortcrust pastry

Preheat oven to Gas mark 4/350F/180C

1. Roll out the pastry to fit the 16 patty tins, or one 9" tin.
2. Fork the cheese until smooth.
3. Heat the butter, eggs and sugar gently in a pan until the mixture thickens, but do not let it boil.
4. Remove from the heat and stir in the cheese.
5. Finally add the dried fruit, lemon zest and almond essence.
6. Spoon into the prepared pastry case/s. Sprinkle with grated nutmeg.
7. Bake for 25 – 30 minutes.

Nutty Apple Crumble

This recipe came from one of the Desborough Junior School teachers in the late 1960s or early 1970s, probably Miss Gutteridge. It was used as a handwriting exercise in school and I have copied it from my original handwritten copy. I don't recall us doing a practical cookery lesson using the recipe, but it is still the recipe I use every time I make crumble, although I usually use an alternative filling. Porridge oats make the crumble have a lovely, crunchy texture. Liz Harris.

For the topping:
4oz SR flour
2oz butter
2oz white sugar
2oz rolled oats

For the filling:
1 lb cooking apples, peeled, cut and cored
juice of 1 orange
4oz white sugar

Preheat oven to Gas mark 5/375F/190C

Filling
1. Grease a two-pint dish.
2. Put half of the sliced apples in the dish and sprinkle on half the sugar. Add the remainder of the apples and sugar. Pour the orange juice over the mixture.

Crumble
1. Rub the butter and flour together in a bowl, until they are like fine breadcrumbs.
2. Gradually add the sugar and oats; mix thoroughly.
3. Sprinkle the crumble mixture over the apple mixture in the pie dish. Put the dish on a baking tray and place in the oven.
4. Cook for 40 minutes.
5. Serve with custard or cream.

Plums in Batter

Can be served hot or cold; there's never any left for cold in our house! Diana Smith.

Yorkshire pudding batter
4oz plain flour
2 small/medium eggs
½ pint milk
pinch of salt
½ oz lard

½ - 1lb of plums (preferably Victoria) – stoned and halved

Preheat oven to Gas mark 5/375F/190C

1. Heat lard in a baking tin; when good and hot pour in the batter mix.
2. Scatter the plum-halves evenly in the batter.
3. Bake for 30 - 40 minutes.
4. Sprinkle with sugar.
5. Can be served hot or cold.

The Frugal Housewife's Plum Pudding

If you wish to make a really nice, soft, custard-like plum pudding, pound six biscuits, or dried crusts of light bread, fine, and soak them overnight in milk enough to cover them; put them in about three pints of milk, beat up six eggs; put in a little lemon-brandy, a whole grated nutmeg, and about three quarters of a pound of raisins which have been rubbed in flour. Bake it for two hours or perhaps a little short of that. It is easy to judge from its appearance whether it is done.

Tipsy Tarts (3 to 4 dozen)

This is a recipe I found in a magazine about 30 years ago, but a friend says that she knows it locally as Butter Tarts. At Christmas they can be decorated with pastry stars as an alternative to mince pies. Jill Freeman

Short crust pastry
Either made with 8oz (250g) flour and 4oz (125g) butter or bought readymade.

Filling
4oz (125g) butter
4oz (125g) sugar
8oz (250g) dried mixed fruit
2oz (50g) glace cherries – quartered
2 tablespoons whisky
3 eggs

Preheat oven to Gas mark 5/375F/190C

1. Roll out the pastry and line the tart tins.
2. Melt the sugar and butter together. This can be done in the microwave, but use a glass bowl!
3. Add fruit, whisky and beaten eggs to the mixture.
4. Put spoonfuls into lined tins. This recipe makes between three and four dozen, but they can easily be frozen.

Whisked Jelly

1 packet jelly (any flavour)
1 small tin evaporated milk

1. Put cubes into a measuring jug; dissolve with a little boiling water. When completely dissolved make jelly up to ¾ pint with cold water.
2. Leave until almost set.
3. Whisk evaporated milk until thick.
4. Slowly stir into the jelly; whisk until thick.
5. Pour into a dish and leave to set.

supper dishes

Apples Stuffed with Goat's Cheese and Leeks (Serves 4)
Pommes Farcies au Fromage de Chèvre aux Poireaux

4 large apples (about 8oz/250 g each), cored
1 cup (8fl oz/250 ml) white wine such as Sauvignon Blanc
1 bay leaf
sea salt and freshly ground black pepper
1oz/30g unsalted butter
white part of 2 large leeks (about 9oz/280g), trimmed, well-rinsed
and sliced
7oz/210g goat's cheese (soft)
2tbs/30ml crème fraîche or double cream
flat leaf parsley leaves to garnish

Preheat oven to Gas mark 5/375F/190C (moderate oven)

1.	Place the cored and prepared apples (cut ring round circumference) in a baking dish and pour the wine round them. Add the bay leaf to the wine and lightly salt the interior of each apple.
2.	Place one tablespoon of the butter and the leeks in a large, heavy-bottomed saucepan and cook, stirring and shaking the pan, until the leeks begin to turn transparent. Add two tablespoons of water, stir, and cover the pan. Continue cooking until the leeks are tender, about 10 minutes, adding additional water if necessary to prevent the leeks from sticking to the pan.
3.	When the leeks are cooked, add the goat's cheese and the cream and stir until all the ingredients are thoroughly mixed.
4.	Season to taste with salt and pepper.
5.	Gently stuff each apple with an equal amount of the goat's cheese and leek mixture, pressing it into the cavity and mounding it on top. Top each apple with the rest of the butter.
6.	Bake in the centre of the oven until the apples are tender and the goat's cheese dark golden on top, about 45 minutes.
7.	Remove from the oven and transfer one apple to each of four plates. Garnish with flat-leaf parsley and serve immediately.
8.	It can be served with green salad and a few small tomatoes.

Baked Bean Tart

Pastry
4oz flour
2oz fat
water to bind

Filling
1 small tin of baked beans
quantity of cooked potato
4oz grated cheese
sliced tomato

Preheat oven to Gas mark 5/375F/190C

1. Line the flan dish with pastry; blind bake.
2. Put in the beans and pile seasoned potatoes on the top.
3. Sprinkle with the grated cheese and decorate with slices of tomatoes.
4. Bake in a hot oven until completely warmed through.

Blushing Bunny (A variation on Welsh-rarebit)

4oz crumbly cheese – grated
2 tablespoons milk
1 teaspoon whole grain mustard
2 egg yolks
2 shakes of Tabasco sauce (optional)
2 firm tomatoes, deseeded and sliced
2 slices of bread

1. Combine the cheese, milk and mustard and gently heat in a saucepan until the cheese has melted.
2. Remove from heat and whisk in the egg yolks; fold in the chopped tomato.
3. Season with Tabasco if required.
4. Toast bread on one side, turn and spoon topping onto the bread.
5. Return to the grill and cook until it starts to brown.
6. Serve immediately.

Cheese and Bacon Snacks

1 packet puff pastry
2 oz cheddar cheese (approximately)
2 oz bacon (approximately)

Preheat oven to Gas mark 6/400F/200C

1. Roll out the pastry to an oblong (12" x 8").
2. Spread the grated cheese and bacon on the pastry.
3. Starting from the long edge, roll up like a Swiss roll. Cut into sliced whirls.
4. Place individually on a greased baking sheet.
5. Bake in a hot oven for 15 – 20 minutes until golden brown.
6. Allow to cool. Heat as required.

Lemon and Sardine Pâté

4 small lemons
2oz butter
2oz cream cheese
1 tin of sardines in oil
black pepper
2 tablespoons lemon juice

1. Cut off the top of each lemon and scoop out the flesh; extract two tablespoons of lemon juice.
2. Blend together the butter, cream cheese, lemon juice and black pepper. Then add the sardines, having first drained off the oil; blend for a few seconds.
3. Put the mixture back into the lemon skins and put in the fridge to chill.

Woolton Pie

The recipe for Woolton Pie was the creation of the chef of the Savoy hotel and named after Lord Woolton, head of the Ministry of Food in 1941. With rationing and the lack of available meat, it was said to be 'wholesome fare'. Jenny Blackwell.

1lb each of diced potatoes, cauliflower, swedes and carrots
3 – 4 spring onions
1 teaspoonful of vegetable extract
1 teaspoonful of oatmeal
top with either potato slices or wholemeal pastry

Preheat oven to Gas mark 3/325/160-70C

1. Cook all the ingredients together in a saucepan for ten minutes with just enough water to cover.
2. Stir occasionally to prevent the mixture from sticking.
3. Allow to cool; put into a pie dish; sprinkle with chopped parsley and cover with a crust of potatoes or wholemeal pastry.
4. Bake in a moderate oven until the pastry is nicely brown and serve hot with brown gravy.

Olive Cake

This was given to me by Francoise with whom we stay in France: that's why it's in metric measurements! When I make it I usually cut it in half and freeze half, cutting it up when it has defrosted.
Jill Freeman

250g SR flour
4 eggs
2dl (200 millilitres) oil (I use olive)
1½ dl (150 millilitres) dry white wine
150g sliced green olives
200g smoked ham (cut into short strips) (or pancetta bacon)
150g grated gruyere (or emmental)

Preheat oven to Gas mark 6/400F/200C

1. Mix everything together and bake for about 50 minutes or an hour.
2. Cut into cubes and serve with an aperitif or as an entrée.

Tips
- I use a tray bake tin which is 12" x 8" x 2".
- It freezes very well.
- For vegetarians omit the ham and use extra olives, perhaps those stuffed with peppers or garlic for extra flavour.

Original Cheddar Biscuits (makes 10)

1½ oz rolled oats
3½ oz plain flour
2oz mature cheddar, stronger the better, finely grated
pinch salt
pinch cayenne pepper
4oz butter diced

Preheat oven to Gas mark 6/400F/200C

1. Lightly grease and flour a baking tray.
2. Mix flour, cheese and seasoning.
3. Rub in butter until it resembles fine breadcrumbs; work to form a soft dough.
4. Knead lightly and roll out to approximately one eighth inch thick; cut into fingers.
5. Bake for 12 – 15 minutes.
6. Serve warm with soup or cold with cheese.
7. Can be frozen for one month.

Pork and Apple Pasties (makes 10 – 12 small pasties)

Pastry
12oz plain flour
3oz butter or margarine
3oz lard
pinch salt
cold water
1½ teaspoons curry paste (optional)

Filling
10oz pork sausage meat
4oz cooking apple
4oz onion
salt and pepper

Preheat oven to Gas mark 6/400F/200C

1. Make the pastry; rest it in the refrigerator for 30 minutes.
2. Finely chop apples and onions. Mix thoroughly with sausage meat and season.
3. Roll out the pastry and cut out 4" rounds.
4. Place the meat mixture on the rounds; fold over and seal the edges.
5. Chill for one hour.
6. Glaze and bake for 30 minutes until golden brown.

Rarebit Puffs

1oz butter
6 cloves garlic, peeled and thinly sliced
3oz mascarpone
2oz finely grated parmesan cheese
2 level teaspoons English mustard
1 x 375g pack chilled ready-rolled puff pastry
1 large egg, beaten
salt and freshly ground black pepper

Preheat oven to Gas 7/425F/220C

1. Melt butter in a shallow pan; add the garlic and cook over a moderate heat, stirring occasionally, until soft and pale gold in colour. Tip the mix into a bowl to cool. Once cool, mix together with the mascarpone and half the parmesan cheese; season with salt and pepper (don't use too much salt as parmesan is quite salty) and set aside.
2. Unroll the pastry and lay it out flat, cut it in four length-wise; then cut each piece into six equal squares: 24 squares.
3. Put a heaped teaspoon of the cheese mixture onto 12 of the squares, damp the edges with beaten egg (milk or water will not seal them tightly enough), then lay the second square on the top of each one. Press tightly around the edges to seal. It is essential that they are sealed or the filling will escape.
4. Transfer the puffs to a baking sheet and brush with the remaining beaten egg. Cut a small slit in the top of each one, and sprinkle with the remaining parmesan.
5. Bake in a pre-heated oven for 10 - 15 minutes. Serve immediately.

Meat dishes

Beef in Beer Sauce

3 – 4 lb brisket (boned and rolled)
½ lb streaky bacon
1 lb onions finely sliced
½ pint brown ale
½ pint stock
1 gill wine (¼ pint)
1 tablespoon treacle
salt, pepper, bayleaf

1. Cover bottom of casserole with bacon.
2. Set meat in the centre with onions on either side.
3. Swill with beer, stock, wine and treacle.
4. Season, cover and cook for 3 hours, in a slow oven, or until the meat is tender.
5. The sauce may be thickened at the end of cooking if required.

Chicken and Mushroom Paprika

1lb chicken breasts
juice of one lemon
6oz sliced mushrooms
chopped parsley
3 teaspoons paprika
1½ oz butter
½ pint cream
salt and pepper

1. Cut the chicken into small thin slices. Put in a bowl with lemon juice, paprika, salt and pepper and stir thoroughly.
2. Melt butter in a large frying pan. Add chicken pieces. Cook over a gentle heat for 10 - 15 minutes, stirring now and then.
3. Add mushrooms. Take off the heat, pour in cream and stir.
4. Return to the heat and simmer gently for one to two minutes.
5. Serve with salad or green vegetables.

Chicken and Fruit Curry

3½ - 4 lb roasting chicken
seasoning
2 – 3 springs tarragon
¼ oz butter
4 tablespoons olive oil
¼ - ½ pint of stock made from the giblets

Curry sauce

1 teaspoon curry paste
2oz butter
1 onion chopped
1 tablespoon green ginger, grated
1 tablespoon coriander seeds, crushed
1 tablespoon ground black pepper
1 dessert spoon curry powder
1 fresh mango
2 bananas
1 dessert spoon flour

¾ pint chicken stock
8 fl oz cream
2 ripe peaches,
2 ripe dessert pears
juice of one lemon
½ lb red and black cherries, stoned
2 tablespoons caster sugar
1 heaped tablespoon desiccated coconut, soaked in a cup of boiling water for 15 minutes and strained

1. Place the tarragon, salt and pepper, and butter into the body of the chicken; rub the outside with the oil; roast for 1¼ to 1½ hours baste and turn from time to time. At the end of cooking the bird should be brown and sticky. Allow to cool.
2. Prepare the sauce, melt the butter; add onions and cook slowly, uncovered until soft. Blend in the spices, and continue to cook for 4 – 5 minutes.
3. Draw away from the heat and add the flour and stock. Return to gentle heat and stir until boiling. Simmer for 30 minutes.
4. Add coconut and water and adjust seasoning to taste; strain. Chill well.
5. Peel and chop fruit, place on a shallow dish, and dust with sugar and sprinkle with lemon juice. Cover tightly with film wrap. Keep in refrigerator until needed.
6. Cut the chicken into bite-sized pieces. Partially whip the cream and mix with the cold curry sauce and mixed fruits; spoon over the chicken.
7. Serve with rice salad.

Chicken and Sundried Tomatoes with Tarragon and Paprika Sauce

5 - 6 chicken breasts
8 tbsp lemon juice
2 tbsp paprika
1 large garlic clove, crushed
1 tablespoon fresh tarragon, chopped
2oz butter
12 - 14 sundried tomatoes
½ pint double cream
salt and pepper
chilli powder

1. Slice the chicken thinly and place in a bowl with lemon juice, tarragon, paprika and garlic. Stir the chicken to coat evenly. Cover and leave at room temperature for 30 minutes.
2. Melt butter over a low heat. Add chicken. Cook gently for 8 - 10 minutes.
3. Meanwhile slice the tomatoes into small pieces.
4. Transfer the chicken to a plate. Bubble pan juices for two minutes to reduce slightly.
5. Remove from heat and stir in the cream. Bring the mixture to the boil, stirring for 2 - 3 minutes or until thickened slightly.
6. Season to taste with salt, pepper and chilli powder.
7. Return the chicken to the sauce; add tomatoes. Stir over heat.
8. Spoon into a shallow serving dish and cover with a lid.
9. May be kept warm for up to one hour in oven at low heat (180C).

Francoise's Courgette Recipe (for two)

1 medium onion, chopped
4 good quality sausages slit and skins removed
1 clove garlic
nearly a full wine glass of white wine or cider
2 medium courgettes, coarsely grated
1 good tablespoon chopped parsley
salt and pepper

1. Fry onion in a little oil until transparent and starting to brown. Add crushed garlic and sausage meat to the frying pan and break up.
2. When it starts to brown, add a little wine until it has reduced, then add a little more until it has all gone.
3. Heat up another frying pan or wok until hot, add a little oil and then quickly stir fry the grated courgette over a high heat until it starts to go soft. Don't cook too long and let it get wet.
4. Add the courgette and sausage meat together with the chopped parsley and serve.
5. It's good with runner beans and crusty bread.

Mediterranean Pasta Sauce

Delicious with tear and share cheese and garlic bread and salad.
Jenny Carr, Pioneer Avenue

2 cloves of garlic
1 small onion finely chopped
½ red pepper
½ yellow pepper
½ green pepper
2 cartons of passata or 2 large tins of chopped tomatoes
2 large mushrooms sliced
2 tablespoons extra virgin olive oil
salt and black pepper
1 teaspoon dried oregano
1 teaspoon dried basil
1 tablespoon tomato sauce (if required)

1. Fry the garlic and onion in the olive oil until transparent.
2. Add the peppers and mushrooms and fry until just soft.
3. Drain any excess oil and then add the passata/tomatoes and seasoning.
4. Cover and bring to the boil and then reduce heat and cook for 15 - 20 minutes.

May be served with pasta, rice or noodles.

Pork Fillet stuffed with Pâté (serves four)

pork fillet
3 rashers of bacon

Pâté
½ lb chicken livers
1 rasher bacon, chopped
2 – 3 mushrooms
1 small onion
bay leaf
2oz butter
½ cup red wine

Preheat oven to Gas 6/400F/200C

1. Sauté all ingredients until cooked. Blend until smooth.
2. Place in a greased tin and cook in the oven for 10 – 15 minutes.

Turn oven down to Gas 4.

Prepare the fillet

1. Trim the fat off the fillet.
2. Slice the top of the fillet and stuff with pâté.
3. Cover the opening with the bacon; tie with string to keep bacon in place. Loosely cover with foil and bake for about 45 minutes according to the size of the fillet.
4. Take the juices from the tin; add one tablespoon of brandy. Serve with slices of fillet.

Rabbit Casserole

1 rabbit cut into portions
4 medium onions sliced
2 – 3 carrots, diced or ringed
2 – 3 potatoes diced or sliced
¾ pint stock
salt and pepper
dried or fresh sage and mixed herbs
(tomatoes, mushrooms or any other left-over vegetables can be added)

1. Fry rabbit in a little pork fat or oil, until golden brown, drain and put into the casserole.
2. Lightly fry the onions, carrots and potatoes and add to the casserole dish.
3. Add salt and pepper to taste; sprinkle with herbs and add the stock.
4. Cook in a slow to moderate oven for 1½ hours.

Sausage Pie (serves four)

This recipe was a regular "holiday treat" for my friend Caroline and me, in the school holidays in the 1970s. It was her mother's recipe: Mrs Vivienne Barton, formerly of Headlands, Desborough. Liz Harris.

900g potatoes
2 small onions
1 pack unsmoked rindless back bacon
454g pork sausages
1 – 1½ tins chopped tomatoes
butter and milk to cream potatoes
a little oil for frying

Preheat oven to Gas mark 4/350F/180C

1. Peel the potatoes and boil them in a saucepan.
2. While the potatoes are cooking, chop the onion and fry it gently, until soft, then place in the bottom of a large casserole dish.
3. Remove rind from bacon, and cut into bite-sized pieces, then fry. Once cooked, place into the casserole dish.
4. Fry the sausages, and put into the casserole dish.
5. Empty the tinned tomatoes into the casserole dish and spread evenly, then top with the creamed mashed potato.
6. Put the casserole dish into a hot oven for 20 – 25 minutes to heat tomatoes through and brown the topping.

Sausage Casserole with Cheddar Dumpling

The dumpling cake is like a hot and juicy ploughman's sandwich.
Sylvia Cank.

Prep time: 30 mins
Cook time: 1 hr 35 mins. Cook in a 4 litre oven-proof casserole dish.

To make ahead: the casserole can be cooked two days in advance; warm through, put in the freshly made dumpling and continue as in the recipe. The casserole is suitable for freezing before adding the dumpling.

Casserole

2 tablespoons suet
12 Cumberland sausages
6 small onions, peeled and halved
1 tablespoon tomato purée
1½ teaspoons cornflour
250 ml red wine
6 cloves garlic, peeled and sliced
1 x 400g tin chopped tomatoes
1 x 25g pack fresh thyme; leaves only
1 x 280g onion chutney

Cheddar Dumpling

275g SR Flour
100g suet
75g cheddar cheese grated

Preheat oven to Gas mark 4/350F/180C

1. Spoon suet into casserole and heat on hob over a fairly high heat. Then fry the sausages for five minutes, or until golden brown; transfer to a plate.
2. Add the onions to the casserole; fry until lightly browned; add in the tomato purée, increase the heat and fry for one minute. Lower the heat and stir in the cornflour.
3. Add the red wine and garlic and bring to the boil; cook for two minutes.

4. Add tinned tomatoes, sausages, half the thyme, half the onion chutney and 50 ml of water. Season, bring to the boil and cook uncovered for 40 minutes in the pre-heated oven.

For the dumpling

1. Mix the flour with the remaining thyme and ½ teaspoon of salt, a good grind of pepper and the suet in a large bowl.
2. Add 124ml of water and mix to a firm dough, adding a tablespoon of water if needed.
3. Split the dough in two and flatten each piece into a 15cm circle.
4. Mix the remaining onion chutney with the grated cheese and place in the centre of one of the circles, leaving a 3cm border.
5. Put the second circle on the top of the first one and seal the edges with the back of a knife; lightly score the top to mark out six wedges.
6. Once the casserole has baked for 40 minutes, remove from the oven and put the dumpling on the top. Brush with a little gravy and then bake for a further 30 – 40 minutes until golden.

Savoury Pudding

Excellent with roast pork, duck or goose.

2 inch slice of bread
½ pint milk
3 tablespoons shredded suet
2 tablespoons plain flour
2 tablespoons oatmeal or porridge oats
3 onions
2 eggs
sage
salt and pepper

Preheat oven to Gas mark 6/400F/200C

1. Peel slice and boil onions until tender.
2. Scald bread with hot milk.
3. Add suet flour, oatmeal and drained onions, to which rubbed sage has been added.
4. Lastly add 2 beaten eggs and seasoning.
5. Mix thoroughly and pour into a meat tin in which a little dripping has been heated.
6. Cook in a hot oven for 40 minutes until nicely browned.

Stuffed Bacon

2 lb joint streaky bacon

Stuffing
½ lb sausage meat
½ bread crumbs
1 teaspoon made mustard
2 oz chopped mushrooms   mix all ingredients together
2 tablespoons chopped parsley
salt and pepper

1. Cut a slit through the bacon from side to side leaving the ends intact.
2. Press the stuffing into the space.
3. Wrap loosely in foil, and put into a pan of simmering water, just enough to cover the joint.
4. Cook for about two hours (30 minutes per pound of stuffed weight plus 30 minutes).
5. To serve, remove rind, and serve with sweet/sharp sauce (redcurrant, orange or Cumberland).

Stuffed Spaghetti Marrow

1 medium sized spaghetti marrow (it will probably have to be home grown)

Stuffing
a tin of good quality minced beef with onions, or a tin of good quality stewing steak
fresh chopped onions
fresh chopped pepper of own colour choice
pinch of dried sage or coriander
2oz fine bread crumbs
Oxo cube
seasoning to taste

Preheat oven to Gas mark 6/400F/200C

1. Mix all the ingredients together, adding a little water to moisten if necessary.
2. Cut the end off the marrow and scoop out the seeds and discard them.
3. Fill the marrow with the prepared stuffing mix.
4. Replace the top of the marrow and secure with a skewer.
5. Heat some fat in a tin; roll marrow in the heated fat, coating all sides.
6. Wrap in foil, and place in an oven-proof dish; cook for 1 – 1½ hours.
7. Slice into ¾ inch slices and serve with grilled whole tomatoes, peas and creamed mashed potatoes.

Swedish Gammon

1 piece of gammon 3¼ - 4 lb
3oz black treacle
½ pint pineapple juice
3 cloves
1½ inch stick of cinnamon
3 tablespoons Demerara sugar
dry mustard

1. Soak Gammon in cold water for 24 hours, rinse and put into a large saucepan ¾ full of cold water. Bring to the boil, removing scum.
2. Add black treacle, cloves, pineapple juice and cinnamon stick and boil for 1½ to 1¾ hours.
3. Allow to cool in juice and when cold pull off the skin.
4. Rub dry mustard over the fat.
5. Mix together the Demerara sugar and ground mixed cinnamon and press into the fat.
6. Put in a hot oven until golden brown. Serve hot or cold.

The Frugal Housewife's Chicken Broth

1 whole chicken
1 cup of rice
1 onion
salt, pepper and nutmeg
finely shredded parsley

1. Cut the chicken into quarters: place it in a pan with three or four quarts of cold water.
2. Add one cup of rice and the chopped onion.
3. Season with salt and pepper and a little nutmeg.
4. Let it stew gently until the chicken falls apart.
5. Shred the chicken; remove the carcass.
6. Garnish with parsley.

Wartime Economy Pie

I don't know where this recipe came from but it must have been for wartime economy use as it would have made a meal for a family from one small tin of corned beef. I usually increase the quantities and make three and freeze them. Diana Smith.

8 – 10 oz short crust pastry
small tin corned beef–sliced
large peeled and par-boiled potato–sliced
small onion chopped
approximately ½ pint Oxo gravy – save a little for later
pepper and salt to taste

Preheat oven to Gas mark 3/325F/160-70C

1. Line a pie dish with pastry.
2. Cover this with alternate layers of corned beef, potato and onion until well-filled.
3. Season with salt and pepper.
4. Pour over the gravy, not quite to the top of the dish.
5. Moisten the pie edge with the gravy.
6. Cover with the remaining pastry.
7. Brush the top of the pie with the left-over gravy.
8. Cook in a pre-heated oven for ¾ - 1 hour.
9. It can be enjoyed hot or cold and freezes well.

Preserves

Chutney

These four recipes from 1966/7 were given to me by Don Turner's mum who lived in Lower Street (related to Oscar Turner, the nurseryman in Gold Street, now the Oak Tree Stores). Bob Martin.

Chutney

¾ lb apples, peeled and quartered
½ lb tomatoes, skinned
½ lb raisins
½ lb Demerara sugar
½ oz mustard
½ oz pepper
½ teaspoon salt
1 pint vinegar

1. Mix well and bring to the boil slowly, stir well, and cook to a pulp. This takes ½ to ¾ of an hour.
2. Bottle in sterilised jars.

Chutney – Apple

1 lb sugar
15 large apples, peeled and cored
¼ lb salt
2 oz mustard seed
¼ lb onion
1 teaspoon ground ginger
pinch cayenne pepper
1 lb raisins
1 clove garlic
3 pints vinegar

1. Boil onions, garlic and apples in the vinegar, until they begin to soften.
2. Add the other ingredients.
3. Mix well and bring to the boil slowly, stir well, and cook to a pulp.
4. Bottle in sterilised jars.

Chutney – Apple and Date

2½ lb apples
1 lb dates
½ lb brown sugar
1 pint vinegar
½ oz mustard seed or dry mustard
1 clove
6 peppercorns
1 teaspoon ground ginger
2 dessert spoons salt
3 cloves of garlic

1. Slice apples, garlic and dates; add the rest of the ingredients and cook slowly for 30 minutes.
2. Then simmer gently until the consistency of jam and a rich brown colour.
3. Bottle in sterilised jars.

Chutney – Gooseberry

2 lb green gooseberries
2 lb brown sugar
1½ pints vinegar
1 lb seedless raisins
1 large onion
1 teaspoon salt
1 oz ground ginger
¼ teaspoon cayenne pepper
½ oz mustard seeds or dry mustard

1. Put gooseberries, raisins and onion through a mincer; mix all ingredients together.
2. Boil for half an hour.
3. Bottle in sterilised jars.

Lemon Curd (makes 1 lb)

2 oz butter
7 oz sugar
rind and juice of 2 lemons
2 eggs

1. Put the butter, sugar, lemon and juice into a thick pan or double saucepan; heat gently until blended.
2. Add the beaten eggs and continue cooking, stirring constantly until the mixture thickens.
3. Strain into a sterilised 1 lb jar and seal.

Marrow and Pineapple Jam

5 lb marrow (prepared weight)
2 large tins pineapple
1 lb sugar to each pound of prepared marrow
1 lemon to each pound of prepared marrow

1. Peel marrow, remove seeds, cut up into small pieces and weigh.
2. Put in bowl and cover with sugar.
3. Cover the bowl and leave to stand for 24 hours. It will produce a lot of liquid and the marrow will shrink.
4. Strain the juice from the pineapple and add the juice of **ONE TIN** to the marrow.
5. Grate the lemon rind and strain the juice.
6. Cut the pineapple into small pieces.
7. Add the pineapple and lemon juice to the marrow.
8. Put on a preserving pan, bring to the boil and add the lemon rind. Boil until the jam sets (about 1¼ hours) adding a little more pineapple juice if the jam becomes too thick.

Piccalilli

4 – 6 lb mixed vegetables: marrow, beans, cucumbers, cauliflower, green tomatoes, and onions
4 pints vinegar
8 oz brown sugar
½ oz mustard
½ oz ground ginger
½ oz turmeric
4 teaspoons plain flour
6 chillies and 6 cloves in a muslin bag

1. Cut the vegetables in small pieces and place on large dishes; sprinkle with salt and leave over night, then strain.
2. Put nearly all the vinegar in a pan and when it boils add chillies and cloves in a muslin bag; add the vegetables, ginger and sugar. Simmer for 15 minutes until the marrow is tender.
3. Mix turmeric, mustard and flour into a paste with the remaining cold vinegar.
4. Add to the pan and boil for five minutes.
5. Take off the heat and when cold, remove the muslin bag, bottle and tie down.

Spiced Pickled Runner Beans (makes 6 lb)

This was a recipe from Sue Starmer of Dunkirk Avenue, donated by Bob Martin.

2 lb runner beans (weight after trimming and slicing)
1½ lb onions chopped
1½ pints malt vinegar
1½ oz corn flour
1 heaped teaspoon mustard powder
1 rounded tablespoon turmeric
8oz soft brown sugar
1 lb demerara sugar
6 x 1 lb jars, sterilised

1. Put chopped onions into a preserving pan with 10 fl oz vinegar; bring to simmering point and simmer for 20 minutes until the onions are soft.
2. Meanwhile cook the beans in boiling salted water for 5 minutes, then strain and add to onions.
3. In a small basin mix cornflour, mustard and turmeric with a little of the remaining vinegar to make a smooth paste; add to the onion mixture.
4. Pour in the rest of the vinegar and simmer for a further ten minutes.
5. Stir in both quantities of sugar until dissolved, simmer for a further 15 minutes.
6. Pot into warmed sterilised jars, seal, label and leave for one month before eating.

Lemonade

5 lemons
1½ lb sugar
¾ oz tartaric acid
1 pint boiling water

1. Peel the rinds thinly on to the sugar.
2. Pour on the boiling water, stir well and leave to cool.
3. Put the acid in a bowl, pour over the juice of the lemons; stir well.
4. Mix together with other ingredients.
5. When cold, strain and bottle.

Lemon and Barley Water

This recipe was always used as a remedy for urinal problems in the last century. Sylvia Cank.

4oz pearl barley
3 lemons
4oz caster sugar
2 pints boiling water

1. Place barley in a saucepan, cover with cold water, bring to the boil and boil for one minute.
2. Drain well and place the barley in a bowl.
3. Using a potato peeler, very thinly peel the rind from the lemon, taking care not to remove any of the pith.
4. Squeeze out and strain the juice from the lemons; cover the bowl and set aside for later use.
5. Add the lemon rind and sugar to the barley; pour over the boiling water and stir well.
6. Cover and leave to stand until quite cold.
7. Stir in the lemon juice, then strain through muslin into a jug; cover and refrigerate overnight.

A-Z Index of Recipes